MIRACLES FORGOTTEN

POEMS

LUKE LEVI

YELLOW LEAF PRESS

EBOOK ISBN: 978-1-956716-13-9

Paperback ISBN: 978-1-956716-14-6

CONTENTS

ACKNOWLEDGEMENTS

Some of the poems in this book were first published in the following places:

"Perfection Is Illusion" (Tiny Seed Journal), "To Live Poetry" and "Nostalgia" (Alchemy and Miracles Anthology, Gilbert & Hall Press), "Tree Light" (Free the Verse, 5 Line Features), "Flowers, Forever" and "History of an Oak Tree" (Dipity Literary Magazine, Issue 4), "Warfield" and "Awaken, Rainclouds" (Heron Clan X Anthology), "Flowers Big Enough To Sleep In" (Wild Roof Journal), "Miracles Forgotten" (Poetry of the Wild Flowers Anthology), "Two Haiku" in the Winter 2024 issue of Humana Obscura, "Crape Myrtle" (Vagus Magazine, Summer 2022)

PERFECTION IS ILLUSION

Give me the sunburned flower,
not the unwrinkled beauty.

Let reality wash the color
from roses so I can cradle
them like seeds in their infancy.

Give beauty no eyes but feeling
caught in the silence of life.

And I will let their bloodless petals fly
from my palms as the wind takes them
back to earth.

RENEWAL

Tell me what the flowers know
to wilt and return each new spring
with no tears about their fall
into the dark warmth of earth.
They must know that slumber
is needed to let silence enter the soul.
Renewal: a constant forever.
Even death mends us; we return
to the source of everything that is.

FAWN

The sun climbed down
from each gold leaf
and stepped its toes
very lightly on the forest floor
to sit with a newborn fawn.

SONG OF WINTER

Feeling a strange unease, I go out
and hear cardinals chirp in the crape myrtle.
The tree is bare in winter. Without leaves,
it has no song of waves when the wind blows.
Wispy clouds are its flowers. Red birds are its song.

The tree lets its red leaves fall to survive winter.
Now it rests. The burden of leaves has lifted.
Now the fallen parts of itself nourish the soil.
The unease also disappears. All that is left
is a song of winter from a cardinal.

HISTORY OF AN OAK TREE

A flower lives fast, and we remember it in winter. A tree grows slowly, and we ignore its history.

This oak tree, born in 1804, limbs low to the grass, watches its world change. A Comanche once sat his back against the tree and carved arrowheads. The world was quiet until others appeared. Wind through trees was a song.

War fell through us, and some craved it. Others wanted to listen to trees in the wind.

A Comanche woman washed her long hair in the shadow of this oak, wondering if the trees have speech. What wisdom they would give.

A RABBIT ATE THE FLOWER I LIKED

The purple beauty was loved so much
by a rabbit that she ate the flower
and said your beauty is now my own.

How can I be angry at the rabbit?
I have stolen honey from bees
and tasted spring and summer in gold drops,

as if I could carry the warm seasons
inside of me, as if I stole beauty
so that I would become its essence.

COLLECTIVE SPIRIT

the collective spirit
how dark it is at times
how lonely it feels
to watch us destroy
and call it peace

walking to the pond
where deer drink beside turtles
this world and that world
like the moon and its reflection
on calm water

MORNING POEM

A sense of hope lingers in the morning light.
This play of life tricks us, but the wall we feel
is like the sky—an illusion that hides stars.

Have you heard we are made of the universe?
Each day there is a silence growing in me,
evaporating everything I have ever clung to.

THE OCEAN'S EDGE

In an ocean of love you drift
in a sailboat on calm waves,
through water so clear you can see
yellow fish in the shallow reefs.

Light drifts and you drink it,
as if you're a flower. Nothing burns,
not even your feet on the sand.
We hear gulls laugh on the shore.

Long ago, they thought the ocean
had an end. They imagined water
drifting off the earth, becoming stars.
The ocean being infinite as love.

my heart is green
covered in forests
full of bird echoes

FLOWERS, FOREVER

Every day the white-haired man plants a flower in his garden. He uses a cane and walks slowly, slumping slightly, on the brick pathway.

Sweet fragrances float in the air from all the thousands of flowers, from local to exotic plants, muted colors to vibrant hues. The air is perfect here, and the cold comes and goes like a swift wind through the hills and mountains. And the stream that divides the garden is slow, as if the old man is the stream itself, taking time to flow to the big river further down the mountain.

The white-haired man gets on his knees. With hands wrinkled as a poppy flower, he begins planting a white rose—the rarest flower he could find—and pats the dirt after he's done.

Then he walks to the stone bridge that runs over the mountain stream and listens.

Some strange feeling comes upon him as if a voice speaks through wind, sun, and water.

Planting flowers was his wife's joy, and now it is his own. A flower daily for his love, every flower part of her. One day he feels he will become the mountain stream giving life to the flowers, forever.

A HOME IN ME

After weeks of dark clouds, I hungered
for the light, and when summer came,
I wished for darkness again.

When sweating my weight,
I wished for cold, and when the cactus
froze to its core, I asked for heat.

When love spoke to me in nature,
I was lost in it, and when sadness returned,
I held it in me.

And after understanding the fall
from a tower I made without support,
I made a home in me.

LANTANA FLOWERS

Lantana flowers—the color of sun—
humming of bees,
breathes whenever the wind
rouses its summer slumber.

RELEASE

An image appears of green trees
so bright that they glow in the sun.
Wind pulls the leaning trees.
They bend in unison, like a buoy.

I pick up a fallen leaf as big as my head.
I trace its veins on the leaf and view my palm:
the same pattern of life.

My perception states this leaf is part of me,
but this is an opinion in my mind.
It could be I am a son of the trees
or consciousness briefly stuck in a body.

If I am silent in the forest, I know
the real teems inside the heart.
Then I disappear, let go, release the leaf.

TREE LIGHT

Broken slants of light
from the forest ceiling
is a form of love
I cup into my hands
to drink.

A DOG WITH BREAD

Today warmth fills the village whose streets lay quiet as a lazy day. A dog walks with bread in its mouth—a gift from the baker. And the smell of the bakery blows in the warm wind and flows through the meandering streets. People still sleep in the houses tucked close together. Tired as the flowers, autumn comes nearer and is red and yellow on the rising hills. Sunlight flows easily, like a day with calm and warmth in the heart. The wind is soft, the air warm, even in autumn. But this season knows no rules, and it abides by its feeling and goes with it. After the dog disappears, its feet clapping on the street, a good silence shrouds the village in the hills and plays with the sun.

TO LIVE POETRY

to live poetry is to walk in a forest
or wildflower field
       without conceptualizing
       with a mindless mind

spot the heart-shaped leaf and the hairs of it
and the red veins of the Turk's cap flower
and see our similarities with nature

we are trees and flowers and stardust
       in human form

mind as a clear sky
think like a flower
       bask in sun or moonlight

all there is to know is in the flower

POND TURTLES

At night, when thoughts travel
to what was before and what is,
I look upon slivers of a silver moon
       on the pond.

Turtles poke their heads from the surface
to breathe the scent of wildflowers.
The past fades like little pond waves
       becoming still again.

AWAKEN, RAINCLOUDS

Wake, clouds, to fall your rain
on the cracked earth. Trees and flowers
hold their small hands to you in earnest.

Your cheeks turn gray, but you journey on,
as if the lands beneath your shadows
are invisible ants.

Soon a rain dance will begin,
as superstition is held dear when hope
is as dry as the air in a drought.

FLOWERS BIG ENOUGH TO SLEEP IN

In a world where blue stars shine at night, the flowers are big enough to sleep in. The mountains are full of fruit of all colors and the sun is so close you can pluck it like a lemon. Still, nothing burns and the rivers are clear as morning dew. Strange birds sing day and night, but under the blue stars, they sing softly to not wake the others who prefer to dream. Under a night of roaming clouds, the flowers laugh while growing in delight.

BLACK ROSE

I wished for beauty, not knowing
it was a breath away: a rose
blooming in autumn.

And when I reached beauty,
I grew tired of it,
as if love were a bore.

I wished for lasting beauty,
but death made the rose
withered and black.

And when I cradled the black rose
laughter fell into me when I
realized beauty never dies.

IF WE WERE FLOWERS

If we treated others like beautiful flowers,
would there be conflict?

Hearts must become uncorrupted
and return to their child souls.

But all this is wishful thinking
as I walk among blooming spring.

These flowers walk about without knowing
they hold the entire universe in them.

OCTOBER

Love falls silently, like a rose petal in the wind. Gentle as fallen light in October, a softness arises in the heart. Leaves scatter on the grass by cooling wind. The oak forest gathers the colors of autumn in its bed. Now the fallen will nourish flowers and trees for when they awake in spring. Today a gentleness washes over the hills and releases love from within.

DIVIDED

Feeling is the only truth,
all else is mist and division.

Listen: the whole oak sings
despite the murky day.

These songbirds echo in the heart
like a good dream remembered.

MEMORY

Memory is a fallen leaf in autumn
buried in the earth
by the stomping of deer hooves,
forgotten by the time
of rising wildflowers.

WARFIELD

Brother, I am the dirt beneath your boots.
Thousands of years I've grown flowers
despite rattles of war disturbing my bed.
See the flower there—a wild thing it is—
popping up from the unmarked grave of a soldier
like yourself, the yellow of it stained by sun.

Brother, I'll give you a home here:
a cocoon of dirt wrapped in warmth
and humming of the earth's core
that will keep you dreaming through violence.
Sing to me that war song you chanted from your
metal god, now that your heart is on the soil.

Brother, they sent you away to die for their wealth.
But I'll keep you safe soon, under stars soon to rise,
in the darkness that will take you,

after the moment when all feels well.
And a flower will grow above you,
so I must ask: What color will be your flower?

ONE DAY

One day all the clocks stopped and we were left with the eternal now. Wars ended and were left in the dust of the old world. Everyone had all their needs met and the birds laughed in the trees and hatred flew away in the wind. Flowers smelled of honey in this new wind. Someone shook our shoulders and said this was a dream and to wake up. We found dreams reality and from our hearts sung softly this tune found within. Everything became clean, little by little, our hearts and our world. We awoke from the dark sleep. Some elders say the dark sleep was not us. We had not yet been born.

THE PART THAT ABSORBS LIGHT

In this dry land of hardened plants
even the leaves are strong as live oaks.
A hard freeze broke oak branches,
but the rest of the tree remains alive
in the time of flowering hills.

Wind takes the leaves in autumn
so that an end can lead to a creation.
A soft rain falls as lightly as morning light
and trees on the hills take on the colors
of summer flowers.

Live oak trunks are like alligator scales.
But the starch-like leaves are soft
if you glide the top with your finger.
That is the part that welcomes the sun.
That is the part that absorbs light.

CRAPE MYRTLE

Frilly white flower—wind-blown—
floats above the cedar; how flowers journey,
scatter color, become wind.

Effortless to be a flower in the wind,
to let Nature pull you home,
always home.

FISSURES

There are fissures in life
where silence and light commingle,
where the soul doubts illusions,
like its reflection on the water.

To define the soul is to let noise
of the world fill the musical silence.
A soul holds the silence close,
like a pillow in a nighttime storm.

And when the fissures open,
walking through to the light
is another way to release the names
that we cling to.

TWO WORLDS

Once, when the world was young and the flowers bloomed brighter than those found in dreams, slowness dug itself a home and mingled with old trees in their morning talk. You may still find it hidden in the wild areas that are far from noise.

There, music is from songbirds, frogs, owls, foxes, bees, and hummingbirds. A stream divides this place but also connects it. A paw print in the mud, beside a turtle who sleeps in its own world.

My world is not the same as yours, like the owl who may only know the night. How can I teach the owl what the sun is?

When the owl refuses to wake early to see the sun fall, it believes there is only the moon and her white glow on the flowers. Still, the red roses become white at night, tinged with the feeling that the other side gives.

THE NAMES OF THINGS

The more I attach to the names of things, the less I live, the less I love, the less beauty I see. Then letting go leads to love. When the essence of life arrives, it is in simple things: nature, love, warmth, beauty. I am not a thing, not a singular being. If the soul is everything, as is nature, then I will disappear into it. I already do this when I listen to wind pass through trees, very softly, as if a messenger hands me a poem, but not through words, through feeling, which can only be felt when the mind disappears and the soul understands. To see only with logic is mindless. The soul has no edge and therefore has everything to give. But to give away what restrains the soul is hard to do. We are too attached to names we invent. To let go is to reach the essence of life.

THE HEART INTERPRETS

the eye only sees so much
the heart interprets
what the eye sees

beauty is perception
some find war beautiful
and crave suffering

the creek passes
over smooth stones
trees sway in wind

my soul and the collective
like a sapphire
below the creek

A SINGLE DROP

Cover me during the dusk of this long dream
with the sea-blue flowers of spring
and burn me to smoke so I can be
the wind's breath.

Let me fall on the heat of a good day
among the passion fruit that raccoons steal
happily while under the white-gold stars of night.

In this heat budding red, marking the end
of this world, give me a drop of honey
for when my body is a withered flower,

as a remembrance of when life
touched me strongly. A single drop
to ease the dusk of life.

THE MORNING AFTER RAINFALL

The cooing dove echoes in my heart, then in the valley. The heart absorbs love first—such is the heart's pull to loveful things—and it reverberates across the hills and valleys. Birdcalls scatter to the village paved in cobblestone streets still glistening from the night rain that had fallen so softly on the rooftops. Houses lay sleeping with dreamers of sun. There is no wind anymore; it blew away in the night, gently, as if it was in no hurry at all to fly away in the valley, like the morning fog casted out by sun. The stream flows through the village, below narrow bridges. You can see right through the water and spot the smooth stones that look dark blue, like the distant mountains. Everything appears to be in wait for something. It will be a day of white clouds that pass slow as last night's rain, slow as dreamful days that loll about in the sun.

I LEFT MY HEART

I left my heart in the flowers.
Who will find it among the blue fields
that stretch to the rivers of spring?

If the wind returns my heart to me
I would only lose it again,
because my soul is everywhere.

After death I will be visiting
all the wonderful places
on this and other worlds,
unattached to anything.

Leave me where seeds fall,
as I'm no more than a migrating
bird passing through this illusion.

LET US LIVE FOR ONCE

let us not go mildly into summer
else we rush through and forget love
in the flowers listening to birdsong

let us stop to bask and live for once
to see the butterfly and bee sharing
what flowers bring to wanderers

let us not ignore the colors of life
and hate imagined things that crumble
far easier than the petals of a rose

let us breathe like a bear awaking
from its long slumber to witness
waterfalls ever flowing to home

BENDING LEAF

Leaves that were once crisp and unbending
on the tree are now mosaics on the ground,
rain-soaked and flexible underfoot,
like soft stones to walk on in the forest.
Near their death—which isn't truly death—
leaves become bendable. They yield to the flow
of what is to come. The leaf becomes the soil,
which is the world, and nourishes the trees.
So one leaf falls to become the entire forest.

MEMORIES OF THE WEST

In the arroyo cracked and shouldered
by creosote and cholla and yellow wire-like grass,
the striped bark scorpion travels
under the stars of Texas

until it stops at moonlight
aglow in a brown pool of water,
a remnant of the last rain,
and drinks before scurrying
away with its tan tail curved like a scythe
that cuts through night.

After it disappears in the desert prairie,
a pronghorn, gray fox, and armadillo
will drink the remaining water
until all that's left are mud-filled memories of rain.

NOSTALGIA

There is a nostalgic feeling to singing crickets at night. It invokes memories, the solitude of night, peacefulness in listening without thought, calmness in the world asleep. An owl hoots on an oak branch, its voice echoes in the valley full of moonlit wildflowers. Does the owl remember when, once she could fly, she was left to venture alone? She remembers and sings her song. She has grown like a tree in her solitude. She too must feel memories pour in from the singing crickets.

THE SUNFLOWER

Gold light sits on the petals of the sunflower.
Raindrops huddle together in its heart
while bees rouse from their slumber
and begin to work in the fields.

The morning rain ends and the day life
in nature wakes to drink and eat from the flower;
this is nature in its constant living:
all these buzzing and humming creatures.

People are no different. They sometimes act
unconsciously, living without slowing down
and enjoying the miracles they don't see.
Oh, and how big they act on this small world!

Like a single flower that knows no others.
But the other sunflowers are not so different

in this field that stretches to eternity: one flower
stares at the soil, the other looks to the sun.

SILENT MOON

The moon has its silence to teach.
The sun speaks through songbirds
who bathe in morning light.

Through the movement of leaves
the light flickers. And the sun's fervor
rushes into cheerful animals.

I wait for the moon and sit with it
while the world drains from the mind.
What's left is the comfortable calm.

MIRACLES FORGOTTEN

In the silver dripping of stars, in little beads of rain on wildflowers, a tunnel opens to let us see new horizons. What is left is the sign of better days, spoken through the water falling from the green stuff of dreams. In the tapping of raindrops on the forest floor, nature lets go of all that doesn't exist. What lives is this feeling now, inside rain and moonlight, in this sweet smell of rain, in the softness of falling water in our long drought. Soon wildflowers will rise up—miracles forgotten—like rain not seen for months, dripping and dripping to the dry throat of earth.

ZAZEN

Why does everyone hurry?
I prefer to watch hummingbirds
chase each other under the slowness of clouds,
with no goal in mind.

I lay about and cloud watch.
Birds sing in live oak trees
as the wind hands me fragrant
scents of earth and flowers.

Softly the wind blows my hair.
My forearms tingle by its touch.
How comfortable it is to be nothing,
nothing at all!

WOMAN OF THE FOREST

A woman in a village looks at small things of beauty with her soul. She grows a garden and walks in a forest on a path that her bare feet formed. Leaves crumble under her steps, softly, as if she is gliding above the world.

Deer walk in the distance and pause to turn their heads at the sound of crushing leaves, but they know the woman's presence. And, after pausing, the deer walk further into the mountain forest, like shadows fading at sunset.

One day the path will be overgrown with ferns and no one will know of this woman. Still, a strange feeling lives in the forest, and you may smile in its presence. Each step is a memory of the past, and feelings of the past remain in the air.

THE GOLDFINCH

the goldfinch
in the live oak
says a word
and I say a word

and her feathers
and my hair
keep blowing
in this cold

and in our silence
we still sing
of this returning
sun

PASSION FLOWER

The tongue of the bee is red with flower sugar.
Dusted with yellow pollen, the bee soars
above the colors it has scattered.

You can taste splendor in deep breathes
of passion flowers, dangling green fruit
which plop to the grass like little worlds
attracting raccoons under the cover of night.

These tasters of passion fruit don't realize
they taste what the sun born.

Waiting until stars come alive,
some taste sun in fallen fruit,
after the bees rest from flower-tending.

MOUNTAIN BIRDS

Anxiety poked me with a knife,
but it was only in my mind.

Now sunlight pokes me with warmth,
and it's felt inside and outside of me,
on the skin and in the soul.

All life is the climbing and falling
of emotions, like birds traveling
through white and green mountains.

I KNOW TIME BY SEASONS

Time is made of colors.
A month is human-made,
and a day watches the sun
to see if clouds will blush.
A year is a mix of all colors.

Winter: The snowy owl, whose
eyes are yellow moons, is high up
in the snow-lined oak. Full
of black stars on her feathers.

Spring: The ruby-throated
hummingbird drinks Turk's cap flowers
and hovers in the air. She stops to stare
at me, even though she is the marvel.

Summer: Record heat, but I still wander
outside as sweat drips from my nose.

Bees circle me. I take photos
of their fuzzy bodies.

Autumn: The Japanese maple
looks burnt at the end of her leaves.
There's another drought. Even now,
nature returns every year.

I see time when flowers return.
Memories pour in. These flowers survived
when the branches of old oaks fell
from carrying the weight of winter.

Relief fills my heart. If such soft things
can live in this harsh world, then I can too.

ODE TO THE BLACK-FOOTED CAT

A desert-roaming cat, heavy as a shoe,
kills her prey sixty-percent of the time,
making this tiny cat the deadliest cat in the world.

The size of her hunger, how large it is!
Twenty miles she can walk, under the cover of night.
Watch as she eats a scorpion, then a mouse.

Look how she grows in solitude.
How immense she feels in the desert of stars,
where a shoe-sized cat is greater than the lion.

THE HEART OF THIS GOOD NIGHT

Under the wisp-like clouds of night
that wrap their linen around the full moon
wind carries white crape myrtle flowers
up into the sky to become stars.

The heart of this good night dances
to crickets ringing in the cool air their songs
among swaying hills of grass and oak
blooming white as moonlight.

STARS LIKE HANGING LAMPS
ON A TREE

starving is the heart that longs
for light outside of themselves

when hope grows as a fire inside
to let the searcher see

shimmering stars
behind the elder oak

as if the stars
hang as lamps on the tree

BLACK FEATHERS DAZED ME

A song sung from a black finch
is more beautiful than the red and yellow
birds who look at rarity as intrusion.

The dark stranger sits on a house
after singing her song and listens
to morning chatter.

She will fly off by herself
and be amidst the dark forest
that hold her dreams.

For what or whom she sings
we will never know. The deep sadness
of her life before is gone.

Her voice is a humming that says:
I am clothed in night so much
that solitude is divine.

LOVE POEM TO NATURE

Something is bursting from me: Call it a love poem
to nature. My heart so sings of this I almost weep.
Basking in this morning sun I feel a growth in me, as
if I am a rising flower seeing sun for the first time. In
this hour, the wind softly rushes through trees.
Blissfully, the songbirds gather above me: an
invitation to sit longer, as I am in the trees with
them. Though when I sing, I sing without words but
with a presence beyond mere being. As if the soul
will leave the body that pulls it to the earth. Come
quickly, everything is happening!

COMMUNING

I was supposed to be a farmer,
to give like spring flowers.

Like my ancestors for thousands
of years, to grow from nature
a life with earth.

Now my words speak to nature,
as if I am communing
with every soul.

A SNOW-DUSTED ROSE

A soft heart, like a flower
that dies and returns each year,
becomes softer after each death.

Have you seen a miracle, as small
as a wild rose, dusted with snow
in its wrinkled petals?

Gentle snow falls on the forest.
So tall are the trees that they disappear
in the white world above.

In the silence there is a calm
that grows in the heart, even as
breath fogs my eyes.

To brush the snow off the rose
is to brush off beauty. After boots
crunch snow, my path will soon vanish.

WHITE CRAPE MYRTLE
FLOWERS

white crape myrtle flowers
ruffled as snow on roses
fall from the tree

wind pulls off the petals
and carries them over
the oak trees

like little white birds
flying up and down
green hills

THE CYCLE

Flowers thought dead
nourish the tree
and so become the tree.

And the deer that died
in the field of flowers
becomes the field.

So when we die we become
greater than what we were;
we become everything.

IMAGINATIONS

The rain is sad only because I think it so.
What beautiful things have I turned to sadness?

The world is our mirror, and so it morphs
based on our moods. Even now, a flower
grows in this extreme heat, basking in it.

But it hasn't rained in months, and yet
I feel as though I must reanimate the rain
for it to save us from our imaginations.

DEER AMONG BLUEBONNETS

Sleeping deer in the meadow lift their faces to the forest edge. Bluebonnets form a bed for them.

Falling asleep from the intoxication of flowers, deer bask in the sunlit field, among the shadows of old oak trees. So old are the trees that they dangle near the grass, like water-soaked flowers.

A wind blows and all the blue flowers rise and fall on the hills like waves. And the deer fall back to sleep, drowsy from breathing in spring.

TO GIVE COLOR

to get away from the world
one must think like a flower
and live in a true state

to give color regardless
of the charred battlefield
surrounding the flower

SLEEPING CATERPILLAR

I don't know why I'm here. Each day, I look at butterflies and caterpillars. Neither of them has questions about life. Maybe we should forget questions and enjoy the flight to each flower.

Forget the mind; we are not that. We are thrust into the world like children, and we leave it like children, still knowing nothing, but we act as if we know. We know enough to live well.

So, I set the caterpillar, who sleeps on the leaf, off the path. Is it a he or she—I don't know; I am just visiting earth—but if I step on the caterpillar on purpose, I am no better than the world destroyers who steal with a smile. Caterpillar, after it rained all day, I wonder if you hid inside the asparagus plant where I placed you.

This caterpillar is my child, like all children. If we care for the lives of only those we know, who will place the defenseless on the gold leaves of autumn?

WHOSE HOME IS THIS?

Home is what we carry inside us.
It is a loving calm. Being aware
of the beautiful things around us,
we see much to be grateful for.
Some are blind to beauty
and so cannot live to their fullest.
Walking around, witness a miracle
here and there. These deer sleeping
on the grass in the forest—how
long have their family line existed?
Before the Comanche roamed?
Before people rose from the dust?
They hold all the wisdom, along
with the trees, as nature grows,
like the feeling of home
in the heart.

FOREST MOVEMENT

Wind rushes through mountain cedar. Branches open as if to allow deer to walk through a door to the forest. Trees sway in a frenzy; their berries are blue clusters clinging to one another for warmth.

Spiderwebs enclose the berries to preserve them. But thick air means rain will fall. Does a spider create webs without thinking of time?

When the trees slow down, the sun falls and a peaceful dark sets in. Flowers take on a new mood. And the pond ripples beside reeds and cricket songs. And the whole forest moves so wildly that it flows back to where life began.

GRANTED LOVE

If you give me your love,
I wouldn't know how to hold it.
Maybe as a feeling carried to a garden,
where flowers make me think of you.

Or when I'm alone in a forest
and a wind causes the hair of my arms
to rise up, as if kissed. That's how
it finds me, your love from afar.

I'd hold your love in me,
maybe as a light, a gift, a poem
that is every love poem I write,
to let it rush through my blood.

A LEAF FLICKERS

a leaf caught the sun in its web
and flew off from the mother oak
in a blue wind

on the leaf light flickered
as it turned in the sky
before falling near the trunk

this bed of grass will be
where creation will begin again
where acorn and mother entwine

MORE BEAUTIFUL THAN ALL THAT RUSTS

The gold leaves of autumn lift up in gusts,
then they fall into the earth to nourish
the roots of trees so that spring will flourish;
this is more beautiful than all that rusts.

The Tree of Life tells us more than many books.
Fallen gold returns in the form of spring.
What the true self wants is to wake and sing.
Outward is not the way the searcher looks.

Every colorful leaf of nature trusts
and knows that there is no death, no ending,
like sheep guided by the shepherd's tending;
this is more beautiful than all that rusts.

SEE THE WIND

The wind pulls off autumn leaves,
knowing the trees need help
changing into their dark clothes:
bareness for their winter sleep.

Strong gusts from the cold mountains
flow up and down these green hills.
You can see the wind through
the swaying trees.

A peaceful sound as the sun sleeps
comfortably on the live oak leaves.
Touch a fallen live oak leaf
and it'd feel like oily skin.

Each day a sign here and there.
No separation in nature: Look at
that tree with so many vines on its trunk,
all climbing together to the sun.

A DEER PRANCING

Upon the green field dotted with daisies,
a deer goes prancing, leaves one forest
to reach the other forest. As she turns,
the deer looks at the white flowers
and sees three other deer come along,
as if the speech of animals is silent
and we have not yet learned language.
We muddle our emotions with words.
Yet poetry is clearer than we realized—
closer to expressions. As if the silence
teaches more than words do.

CHANGING GRASS

Today, sunlight falls into the grass,
staining it gold. Someday a hard freeze
will sharpen the blades of grass,
and some will walk on it, crunching
under their shoes. For now, it's gold.

Bright as the first light above the hills.
Silent as early morning, when deer
have their whispers shone in the air.
The grass comes and goes, from gold
to frost-white, deer-tan, and green.

Each has a feeling and sound to give.
But their songs, like the trees,
are best heard from close by.
Today, sunlight falls into the grass,
staining it gold. For now, it's gold.

STILL LAKE

It's such a still lake that the bow of the canoe
seems to fold the water up, as if it's a tablecloth
being pushed out by a finger. The oars lift
the silence of the water, dripping of it.

An eagle swoops down, as if conjured.
It clutches a fish from the shallows,
flaps its wide wings, and disappears
behind the mountain of pine.

The water settles to a blue mirror.
It's so still that the sun on the lake
perfectly reflects itself while clouds
slowly cross the illusion to the other side.

THE SOURCE OF SINGING

The stars fall on me in the meadow
beside a dark creek.

The fighting world stops and singing crickets
celebrate in hidden places.

If I would try to find the source of singing,
I would never find it.

Instead, I embrace the stillness of night
and listen to water.

This world is like a mirror, although
I can't see my face on the creek, only stars.

like a fallen leaf
I also will become
the earth

WHAT TREES TEACH

Burdens lift among the trees and fade forever, or for
a moment, as all things must fall, much like leaves
in autumn. Otherwise, nothing would exist.

The tree lets go to carry on. The sun falls to give
nature rest. And nature is endlessly reborn
and includes us. We are neither above nor below it.

When we go into a forest, there is no separation.
We dissolve what we cling to and become ourselves,
but only when we release what holds us back.

OREGON SCENE

A felled tree grows mushrooms from its mossy trunk. A vine blankets another tree's grave, as if nature also has her customs.

Nearby, the furled fern begins to open; soon it'll be a large green umbrella for the fallen trees.

The first tree is a bridge over the mountain stream. Water jumps over smooth stones, before becoming a waterfall and joining the Columbia River.

The water needs stones to make music. The fallen tree needs a vine or mossy blanket to keep warm. Each part of nature is joined with another part, inseparable.

POPPY FLOWER

In its cupped hands, the red poppy flower
holds a sleeping bee. Listen closely
and you can hear snoring—subtle as light
falling between clouds.

Tired from pollination, this bee
has tasted all the garden's colors.
From his work, the world blooms
more beautifully—does he know it?

Wind pushes fragrant flowers to taste,
as if nature is saying to linger and find
what is good in the world, like the bee
spreading flowers in love.

ON MY WALK TO THE POND

Walking into the forest,
cedar limbs hold their hands
against my chest as I enter its heart.
Turning back, light pours down
to illuminate verbena flowers,
as if they're purple lanterns
guiding the way to the pond.
In the fading light, wind moves
the top of the trees, swaying
like hair being played with
by a lover. In the open field,
beyond the forest edge, deer
look up from the field of yellow
flowers and then walk on,
as if I am one of them.

HOW FLOWERS BECAME WEEDS

following my lost soul
it led me into a field
overrun with thorny wildflowers

I ignored the beautiful flowers
and thought of thorns as hell
and so named these plants 'weeds'

YELLOW BUTTERFLY

A big yellow butterfly was the light that day.
She sprang from the red flowers shaped like tea cups.
The butterfly drank up the last remnants of summer,
flapping her wings slowly as a near soundless song,
building up to a big moment.

After she was full, she flew over the cedar trees,
climbing on a winding ladder to the sun,
blowing up by early autumn gusts.
As if nature took a deep breath and guided
the butterfly—with a gentle hand—to that next place.

VITTLES

Like people, songbirds go out
in the cool morning to sing,
before their morning vittles.
They speak their language
that we still don't know yet.
Sometimes human language
is an obscure murmur,
a whisper mistaken for wind,
like a finch asking for love
yet it comes out as a song.

on a lonely road
you may find yourself happy
alone at sunset

SLEEPING BEE

Rain rarely fell in those days, so when it did, people were happy. They would listen to rain drip down the leaves of trees and tap brick roads. Even birds sang in the cover of forests.

When the rain ended, you felt a little sad. But then you would smell the air, sweet like flowers, and bumblebees would come out from hiding.

Where do bees go in the rain? And you'd wonder and maybe search for their hiding place during the next rain.

There was a flower, shaped like a bell, and a little bee was inside it, sleeping like a cat after eating. I remember everyone came out to see it. In that place, there was only good news. A reporter took a photograph of the sleeping bee in the bell flower, and we read about it that week.

I don't know why we remember such a small

thing. Maybe it wasn't so small. It feels like that memory is from another planet, not my own.

BLUE MOONLIGHT

Blue star among sleepy clouds,
you have graced us with a faint light,
shining silver on grass valleys.
Jumping from dark forests,
behind a translucent cloud veil,
where do you scurry to?
A deer drinks your silver face.
Lifting her head, the lake drips
from her nose, watering the moon.

midwinter
the forest trees
darken from rain

December—
a cold wind
dances the trees

a dusting of snow
the raven shakes it off
in each caw

SONG OF LIGHT

Wandering among the trees, names are forgotten. Wind and sun fall through me while a goldfinch sings above my head. Leaves hop down the hill; I pick one up and the wind tells me to let it go—so I've read. The world comes and goes, all seen before. But somehow it seems to be brighter. Even the finch holds a song of light.

AWOKE TO A DREAM

When awake, it was still a dream.
What else explains these songbirds
and the bee landing on my hand?

Beauty in a white flower
ruffled as a lover's hair in the wind
shows life in its ethereal nature.

The hands try to grasp it
but the child feels it fully
without knowledge.

One forgets as the years pass
that seed and withering flower
are neither beginning nor end.

All the illusions plain in sight
give birth to a hidden sun.
All the names are mist.

Awoken from a long dream,
the wordless speaks in silence,
when the search ends.

WHAT AM I?

my reflection on the pond
is faceless as the trees

where is my name in nature?
I dissolve into quietness

let the wind take names
as it does to fallen leaves

THE SOURCE OF BELIEF

let go of your beliefs
then try to find them in silence
without thoughts

do trees whisper beliefs?
does the universe
and soul align?

while sitting still
birds gather above me
thinking me to be a tree

RUSH

if you wish, we can sink into the sky,
forget rules and be infinite as galaxies,
live as poetry, as a tree, then be a mountain
or an entire planet, sleep through life
like a cat (cougar or house cat?), then
laugh and be like children not caring
about made-up things that most cling to,
let go and live for once—or forever.
oh, I'm tired too, why? I always sleep
enough, but it's deeper than sleep,
we're being pulled somewhere,
by invisible hands, as if it's all melding
into a world, like this little one,
the unknown will remain unknown,
I've come to accept it, like the cat
chasing the butterfly, she never catches
it but wishes to fly too, like us,
to rush upwards

ALL THAT SHINES

Nothing truly belongs to me.
What I love flows through
and out of me as wind.

Gathering and releasing
leaves in the air,
like a raven finding all that shines
to be beautiful.

UNDER THE SPRING MOON

Under the spring moon
whose blush falls gentle
on still waters of a dreaming pond,
a white heron walks like a crusader
surveying the crumbling world
before flying away on wings
that flap with no sound,
like wind-blown flowers
that sing without words.

ODE TO WATER

Water has its many songs.
A river jumps over river stones, tries to fly,
but sometimes it eases and walks around boulders.
Sometimes it is creative and creates underwater
caves or canyons or swamps or lakes.
It fans out on the white sand beaches,
then makes its way to another continent.
Sometimes it's quiet in the deepest oceans,
where light is so scarce creatures make their own
or need no eyes and use touch instead.
Water becomes the biggest part of the person,
gives them life and now and then takes it.
Sometimes water falls from high up,
down a cliff, when it wants to join a river or sea.
When it is rain, it becomes the earth,
sinks down into home—home which is everywhere
it wishes to be.

the world is absurd
but I still cling to its flowers
like a bee drunk on spring

WINTER CATERPILLARS

Morning light after a night drizzle
bounces off every pebble of rain.
On trees: globes of water like diamonds.
Today it will be 20 degrees warmer,
on December 9. The caterpillars I saw
yesterday were still alive, somehow,
and they may even become butterflies
in winter. Then it must feel strange
to come alive in the cold. You awaken
to a cold world, but would you
know it's cold? When they awake
from their sleep, do they remember
their past life as a caterpillar?
Do they remember the Texas heat?
Some hopes survive as caterpillars
still alive after cold spells. I search
for signs in nature and find them

everywhere. In a warming world,
I still see beauty in strange places.
Let this hot December day give birth
to what we love. Since love returns
after the remaking.

STAY

loud world
quiet trees

in the wind
leaves fly off
branches sway

letting go
and holding on
to what must go
and stay

THE FIRST PERSON WHO SAW THEMSELVES

Every day is a different sun,
a new feeling, a changing world.
All reflects the mind, like the moon
on water.

If I had not known my reflection,
and one day, for the first time,
looked at my reflection on a still pond,
I would find myself to be a stranger.

FOLKLORE

The old man dreamed he was a hawk and saw through its eyes all of the world from above: all the waterfalls flowing down the green mountain sides of Norway to the sea. He ate rabbit and tasted the metallic taste of blood, and knew nothing of good and evil. Then he dreamed he was a tree, watching people sit beneath his shade, but over the course of thousands of years. From there, everything distorted. Time flew so fast that he saw the rising and falling of each civilization, the end and beginning of planets, of infinite stars and galaxies, and he felt small and unimportant but also part of it all. When he awoke, he visited his wife's moss-covered grave, under the shade of a lone tree, in the mountains from which he lived in their shadow. In spring, flowers grew where none had lived before, and he felt his wife was in them and that the tree would one day be him.

the end is a beginning
from their grave
daffodils bloom

THE RIGHT HOUR

The earth has a memory.
At the right hour the flower wakes,
sensing warmth in darkness.

From the flower's grave in autumn,
life resumes in spring.
We see life after death each year.

Rain falls down each earthly pebble
and speck of dirt, dripping
like rain in a cave.

The seed knows the hour.
The unborn flower waits in its pod,
sleeping, until born again.

BEGGARS AND TAKERS

It is a splinter of love; the light shining
in a million fragments through the forest trees.
When thoughts subside, presence
becomes a house of light. Love captures
me in its net, though love is not external;
it is inside me, emanating as a sun.
Once crawling, now taking flight,
a great feeling consumes me.
Out of the dark night, coyotes
pay me no mind. I am one of them.
And the possum family passes by;
I am one of them. And the faces
on sidewalks, and the beggars
and takers of the concrete world,
I am one of them. A sea of love washes
over beaches where love may begin,
out of the dark night of infinite stars.

The northern lights also reach us;
we enjoy the colors in silence.
If we used words, we'd muddle the feeling
of love for the mystery and beauty
of everything.

THANK YOU

Thank you for reading my poetry book. I hope you enjoyed it!

If you don't mind, leaving a review would be greatly appreciated. Reviews help new people find my books. They are extremely helpful for an independent writer like myself, and I appreciate each one.

You can also leave a review on Goodreads or, if you bought this book from an online store, the store's website, or both.

In the meantime, before my next poetry book comes out, you can find me on most social media sites. You can also email me at: lukelevi4@gmail.com

Thank you again,
    Luke Levi

ABOUT THE AUTHOR

Luke Levi is a poet and photographer. His poems can be found in more than twenty magazines in the US and UK. Most of his photos depict the Texas Hill Country. You can find him on social media @lukelevipoet and also at lukelevi.com.

facebook.com/lukelevipoet
instagram.com/lukelevipoet

OTHER POETRY BOOKS BY
LUKE LEVI